LOVE

THE DRIVING FORCE OF LIFE

VIVEK GUPTA

The Driving Force of My Life

my family

my Love

347

Contents

Contents

Contents

Contents

Preface

Love is often seen as a force that brings joy and fulfilment, but this book is not about that kind of love. Instead, it delves into the complex, often painful reality of love—a reality where relationships drift apart, hearts are broken, and healing feels distant.

In the first few poems, I explore love's true essence—the purity and strength it holds in its ideal form. But soon, the focus shifts to how love fades, how connections weaken, and how we are left grappling with the detachment of someone we once held close. This phase of loss and heartbreak forms the core of this collection, reflecting the emotional depths we sink into when love no longer stays.

Yet, this is not a story of despair. It is a story of resilience. As the poems progress, they move beyond the pain, exploring the quiet strength we find within ourselves—the hope that, even after the most profound loss, healing is possible. The final section of this book celebrates the rebirth of love, the courage to trust again, and the possibility of starting anew.

Love is, indeed, the driving force of life. Not because it is always beautiful, but because it teaches us to endure, to grow, and to find light even in the darkest moments. I invite you to walk this journey with me—a journey through love's highs and lows, its sorrows and its second chances. Perhaps, in these verses, you will find echoes of your own story and a reminder that even after love fades, it can bloom once more.

GENTLE REMINDER !!!

Dear reader,

Please SMILE.

Life is too short to remain sad.

1. What is Love?

What is love, if not a spark,
That lights our way when life turns dark?
A gentle touch, a steady guide,
A quiet strength we hold inside.

It's in the eyes that understand,
In holding tight, not letting go of a hand.
It's found in whispers, quiet and true,
In every "me" that turns to "you."

Love is patience when tempers rise,
The strength to stay, to compromise.
It's not in winning, but standing near,
In sharing smiles and wiping tear.

It's the courage to heal, to mend,
A journey walked with a loyal friend.
It's in the flaws, the scars we show,
In every "yes" when the heart says "no."

What is love, if not the grace,
That lifts us up in life's embrace?
It's the home we find, the peace we crave,
A light that shines beyond the grave.

2. The Strength of Love

Love isn't just a fleeting touch,
It's the force that lifts and restores so much.
In dark moments, when shadows stay,
Love finds the light and clears the way.

It holds you close when storms arise,
A gentle shield beneath the skies.
Through trials faced, through battles fought,
Love teaches lessons pain has brought.

It builds a bridge when walls appear,
It calms your doubts, it quells your fear.
No force on earth can break or bend,
The power of love—our truest friend.

3. Beyond the Poet's Dream

They say love is sweet, gentle, kind,
A poet's dream, a heart's rhyme.
But love, in truth, can cut and heal,
A fire that scars, yet helps you feel.

It's not just stars in the skies above,
But hands that hold when problems grow.
It's facing storms, the darkest nights,
And finding warmth in softer lights.

But then, false love comes into play,
With empty words that fade away.
It whispers close, then slips like sand,
And leaves you hurt, too weak to stand.

It shows what trust can tear apart,
How broken promises scar the heart.
How even love, when cold and fake,
Can steal the joy it seemed to make.

Yet still, we hope, and through the pain
We search for love, again and again.
Beyond each wound, beneath the sky,
A love that waits, won't let dreams die.

Not made of words poets may say,
But built on truths that will not sway.
A love that grows, that stays for years,
A shelter found beyond our fears.

So keep that hope alive each day,
For real love always finds its way.

4. The Lost Essence of Love

When love was first born, it was so bright,
A sacred flame, a purest light.
It healed the soul, it mended the scar,
A magic that felt like wishing on a star.

But time, as always, played its hand,
And love bent low to meet demand.
No longer pure, no longer whole,
We traded its heart, we sold its soul.

Love turned to deals, to fleeting games,
A mask of desire, a borrowed name.
It's tainted now, by greed and lies,
A fragile bond that quickly dies.

Few still seek its ancient grace,
A love that time cannot erase.
But many now, in haste, embrace,
A shallow form, an empty space.

The magic fades as shadows grow,
True love's a path few dare to go.
Yet for those who hope, who dare to believe,
The true magic of love, they'll one day receive.

5. Forgotten Truth

A long time ago, life was clear and true,
We loved each other and used what we knew.
But as years slipped by and the world grew cold,
People traded warmth for things they could hold.

Now, we cherish objects, shiny and bright,
And treat each other with less and less light.
We've started loving things that fade,
While using hearts in a careless trade.

If only we'd remember what we've lost,
The simple truth and its quiet cost.
For love was meant to heal and give,
Not buried under things that don't live.

6. A Friend's Query

A friend asked me, "Why do you care so much?"
I paused and said, "It's like a soft tender touch.
In a world so cruel, where kindness feels rare,
Someone must love; someone must care."

I choose to stand, though the path can be dim,
To be the light when hope seems slim.
For in the depths, when shadows crawl,
Love is the whisper that beckons us all.

It's the warmth in the chill of a lonely night,
A flame that flickers, yet burns so bright.
For in the end, when shadows fall,
Love is the answer; it matters for all.

7. The Choice

A true soldier stands, not for the glory or fame,
But for love, for the bond without shame.
In battles and pain, he cleans the dust,
For those he loves, for the bond of trust.

Not driven by glory or thrill,
But by the quiet strength, the unshaken will,
To guard, to hold, to shelter from harm—
To keep his loved ones safe and warm.

And when the heart beats for someone dear,
You'll find the courage to stand right here,
To fight, to fall, to rise again—
A promise kept, through joy and pain.

So, choose the path that feels like light,
The one that's worth each day, each fight.

8. A Promise of Faith

Believe me,
My heart is true,
At every moment,
I'll stand by you.

Believe me,
When shadows dance,
Through every challenge,
I'll take the chance.

Believe me,
In the darkest night,
With every heartbeat,
I'll be your light.

Believe me,
Cast away your fear,
In the quiet whispers,
I'll always be near.

Believe me,
As the seasons fly,
In every sunrise,
I'll never say goodbye.

Believe me,
Anytime — Any day,
I will stay with you and never run away.

Believe me,
What I say is 100% true,
I want to live, with you, for you.

Please Believe me...

- a request

9. The Myth of Being Busy

Being busy is just a tale we tell,
A way to hide what we know so well.
It's not the hours that keep us apart,
But the choices we make, right from the start.

To say "I'm busy" means I chose this way,
Something else took my time today.
It's a matter of what I choose to see,
What holds my focus, my energy.

So when I say I'm busy, please know it's true,
I'm simply doing what matters more than you.

10. Echoes of a Fading Bond

Replies became slower, priorities changed,
Chats grew shorter, with distance rearranged.
Situations blamed, yet hearts drift apart,
Unspoken words, tearing at the heart.

What once was close now feels so far,
A fading light, like a dying star.
In the silence, memories ache,
Reminders of what's now hard to take.

Will time heal what's been torn away,
Or leave us broken, lost on the way?
Perhaps the space deepens the scar,
And love becomes a wound too far.

The echoes of what used to be—
Now lost in pain, lost in me.

11. If You Walk Away

If my tears alone bring you such pain,
How will you bear my blood's crimson stain?
A single glance, and when I'm away,
Your restless heart begins to fray.

Yet you speak of leaving, walking free,
Of turning your back, abandoning me.
If I were gone, my breath no more,
Would your soul not ache at its very core?

I'd crumble, yes, my life would cease,
But tell me truly, would you find peace?
Apart from me, could you survive,
Or would you too feel barely alive?

This bond we share, fragile yet strong,
Would leaving not feel painfully wrong?
For in my absence, you'd come to see,
Living without me—isn't living, truly.

12. Respect What We Share

Respect my feelings, respect what we share,
The bond we've built with so much care.
For someday, you might come to see,
You won't meet someone quite like me.

These moments we have, rare and true,
Are threads of life, tied tight through you.
So hold them close, don't let them slip,
Our connection's deeper than words can grip.

13. Burden of Truth

Every truth feels like a lie,
Each hidden truth, left to die.
We build a world on shifting sand,
Where nothing real can truly stand.

Faking smiles, hiding tears,
Drowning in our silent fears.
We lost ourselves in endless show,
What's real, we may never know.

The weight of lies, so hard to bear,
Truth is lost, does no one care?
I wonder now, with a heart so sore,
Are we doomed to fake forevermore?

Each step we take, lost in the night,
Chasing shadows, losing light.
I ache inside, can't help but cry,
What future holds when truths all die?

14. Regret's Silent Burn

Whatever I do, whatever you say,
It's just a matter of time.
Everything will decay,
But your regrets will stay.

No matter, where you go,
Doesn't matter, how much you try,
The very moment you sit back relax,
That regret will come again,
Burning your happiness into its invisible flame.

Still, you are not doing anything about it,
What you are thinking, is it a game?
Have you admitted it,
Or it's just a lack of shame.

15. At the Edge of Goodbye

How unfortunate we are,
To meet at the very last hour,
When all that's left to say is
The painful word—goodbye.

We once shared dreams, hopes, and time,
Now, they fade like a forgotten rhyme.
In silence, we stand, hearts heavy, torn,
Wishing for moments that could have been reborn.

The hands that once held, now let go,
As if the warmth was never meant to grow.
In the final glance, I see the ache,
The love we lost, the path we couldn't take.

But here we are, at the edge of it all,
No words to catch us before we fall.
Just the weight of memories and the pain of this night,
As we walk away, out of each other's sight.

16. Will You Miss Me?

I miss you more than words can say,
In the quiet nights and bright of day.
Your absence lingers, a silent pain,
I wonder, will you miss me, too, again?

In every thought, you're still so near,
Yet you're so far, and I feel the fear.
Of losing moments we used to share,
I miss you, but do you even care?

When the world feels heavy, and I'm alone,
I long for you, to call it home.
I miss you with each beat of my heart,
But will you miss me when we're apart?

I carry this question, day and night,
Hoping someday, our paths will unite.
I miss you deeply, more than you'll know—
But will you miss me, when I let you go?

17. Shattered Trust

I loved her deeply, stood by her side,
Through every storm, with every tide.
I gave her my all, my heart, my soul,
But now I'm left to mend what's no longer whole.

She vanished like mist, without a sound,
Leaving my trust scattered on the ground.
She broke me apart, left me undone,
Now I gather the pieces, one by one.

I fear the day someone steps near,
To shatter what's left, confirm my fear.
Will my fragments dissolve, fade to none,
Lost forever, under a crueller sun?

I'm sad, I'm scared, I stand alone,
In this quiet pain, a world unknown.
But in this solitude, I'll learn to stay,
Guarding my heart, come what may.

18. Masks Upon Masks

Everyone wears a hidden face,
A mask that shifts from place to place.
Most of what you think you know,
Is just a part of their crafted show.

Love and trust, they trade with ease,
Honesty fades like autumn leaves.
And when you're no longer of use,
They leave, without a single excuse.

I've been traded, I've been sold,
By hearts that turned both harsh and cold.
But one day, their masks will fall,
And the truth will echo through it all.

19. Hidden Scars

I kept the truth locked deep inside,
Fed it with sorrow, let my heart divide.

Each hour slipped by, lost in decay,
As I chopped at my soul, bit by bit, day by day.

Blinded by pain, I crafted my sorrow,
Building my own grave, unsure of tomorrow.

20. Let Me Fade Away

If I shatter and fall one day,
Promise me, you'll look away.
Don't try to piece my soul again,
Don't bear the weight of my silent pain.

Let me go; it's time to be,
A shadow lost in eternity.
No battles fought for a life now done,
Let me dissolve beneath the sun.

Bury these fragments, deep and low,
Where no winds stir, where memories won't grow.
Burn my essence, every trace,
And cleanse the air with purifying grace.

Don't weep beside my lonely grave,
No tears to bind, no heart to save.
In the quiet, let your sorrows part,
For no one's there to mend your heart.

This end I seek, a chosen plight,
To vanish in the endless night.
Erase me from your every thought,
Let the world forget the battles I fought.

I beg of you, let my presence cease,
And in this silence, find your peace.

• 23 •

21. When Hopes Shatter

Hope's break, a pain so deep,
Far beyond what hearts can keep.
For hopes are born where love resides,
In hearts where trust and care collide.

When those you cherish let hopes fall,
It's not just dreams—they break it all.
The heart that held them, bruised and torn,
Feels the sting of love, now worn.

That's why Hope's fall leaves a scar,
A wound that aches, both near and far.
It hurts much more, the silent ache,
For when hopes shatter, hearts will break.

22. The Weight of Karma

One day, tears will stain your face,
A silent storm you can't erase.
Pain will knock, and troubles flow,
In life's harsh trials, you'll come to know.

It's the loop of karma's endless spin,
The echoes of deeds done deep within.
For seeds once sown, we're bound to reap,
In restless nights, no peaceful sleep.

Time, once gone, won't turn around,
The truth will strike without a sound.
You'll face the past, with no place to go,
For, in the end, we all must grow.

23. The Stars Within

They say we choose to let sadness stay,
To walk in shadows, to drift away.
But joy, they claim, is ours to hold,
A treasure we grasp, a story told.

Yet happiness bows to time and fate,
A fragile guest at life's front gate.
While pain, like stars, forever glows,
Hidden by light that briefly shows.

In the daylight of good times near,
We lose the sight of what we fear.
But stars don't fade; they bide their time,
Returning with the night's soft chime.

So is it strange, this cosmic plan,
Where joy is fleeting, but pain withstands?
Perhaps it's life's way to remind us all,
That even in light, shadows never fall.

24. A Question to Life?

If I am love,
Made of love,
Born to give, to rise above.

Then why, in this vast worldwide,
Was I left alone, unloved inside?

If love flows in each breath I take,
Why am I left with hearts that break?
A soul crafted to care and hold,
Yet finds itself alone and cold.

It hurts deep inside,
To see the truth so hard to hide.
Everyone needs you, in their own way,
Yet no one truly asks you to stay.

Invisible in their world, you remain,
Always there, yet left in pain.
Needed by all, but cherished by none,
A silent battle that's never won.

In quiet moments, you feel the ache,
Of giving so much, still, there's nothing to take.
Empty and worn, you stand alone,
A pillar for others, with no warmth of your own.

25. If I Am Innocent

If I am Innocent, why must I cry?
Let the pain in my heart slowly die.

Take away the darkness & the tears, that I hide,
And bring some colour to my empty side.

You know, I was innocent,
I remain so still,
By heart, by soul,
Through every trial and will.

Innocent, whole,
Through life's vast tread,
And God, you know,
What's left unsaid.

26. The Silent Question

Why, dear God, is there so much pain?
Why do we walk through endless rain?
If You made life, why fill it with tears,
Why make us carry these heavy fears?

Why are the nights so cold, so long,
With no bright stars to keep us strong?
Why can't the darkness hold some light,
Why is it so hard to make things right?

Why does love leave, leaving us torn,
Why do hearts break, tired and worn?
If You gave hope, why is it so shy,
Hiding away while we question why?

I seek the answers, I search the skies,
But silence greets my pleading cries.
Still, a small voice whispers, soft and near,
"Hold on, the light will soon appear."

But when, dear God? And how will it be?
Will this darkness ever set me free?

27. The Battle Within

I fight a war within my chest,
A restless heart, a mind distressed.
My brain commands, "Let her go,"
But my heart whispers, "No, no, no."

These memories, both sweet and sore,
Are mine to keep, forevermore.
They bear her name, they tell our tale,
A love once strong, though it may pale.

No one can claim what we once had,
Not joy, not pain, not moments sad.
They're etched in me, they're wholly mine,
Our shared past, frozen in time.

So let the heart and mind collide,
Her essence stays, I won't divide.
For in this fight, I've made it clear,
Her memories will remain right here.

28. The Illusion of Choice

Life doesn't always let us choose,
But when it does, we can't refuse.
Pick wisely, at the right time,
Or face the cost of a fatal climb.

Sometimes, the options we see
Are heartbeats or breath—what will it be?
Choose the heart, and breath may fade,
Choose the lungs, and love's betrayed.

No matter the path, the end's the same,
A silent gift in life's cruel game.
For fate will write its final say,
And tears will fall, come what may.

In those moments, you'll come to know,
Prayers can't halt the sorrow's flow.
And as the truth begins to weigh,
The soul starts to crumble, day by day.

29. The Day I Leave

One day,
I will walk away.

One day,
You'll search for me in every shadow,
But I won't be there to stay.

One day,
You'll have the world in your grasp,
Yet feel the weight of my absence—
A silence too vast.

One day,
You'll confront the mirror of truth,
And see the cracks you etched in my youth.

That day,
You may beg, you may plead,
But no force in the universe will halt my need.

For you consumed the light within my core,
Turned my glow to darkness,
Left me aching, sore.

Yet, even now, in the quiet of the night,

My battered soul whispers:
"Forgive, despite the blight."

But forgiveness, too, will drift away,
When I choose to leave on that fateful day.

30. If Only You Had Waited

If only you had held on, just a little more,
If only you had searched my breaths to their core,

Perhaps, you wouldn't need to dig so deep,
Nor bury love where shadows weep.

In hurry, you silenced a heart so true,
Unseen, unspoken, but it still beats for you.

31. Her Joy, My Prayer

If my pain grants her delight,
Then, O Lord, keep her world bright.

Her happiness, I won't deny,
Even if it means I quietly cry.

If distance is the price I pay,
I will step aside, come what may.

Let her find peace, far from me,
For love asks no less, selflessly.

32. Alone in the Sea of Pain

Whenever someone asked about my heart's state,
I lied, knowing the truth would be too late.
The pain I carried, buried deep inside,
Was mine alone—no one to confide.

With each passing day, my world fell apart,
I wore a mask, hiding a broken heart.
The truth was simple, but hard to see—
That no one was left, not even me.

I drifted through life, alone and lost,
Caught in the storm of a pain that won't cost.
The sea of sorrow swallowed me whole,
As I searched for peace, but lost my soul.

And now I know, as the truth becomes clear,
No one was close enough to hold me near.
Alone I stand, in this quiet despair,
Drowning in silence, with no one to care.

33. The Price of Victory

I've climbed to the highest peaks,
Won battles that time itself seeks.
Held the world in my trembling hands,
Yet failed where no one understands.

In your eyes, a universe remains,
A love untouched, breaking chains.
The victories I've claimed turn cold,
For your warmth was worth more than gold.

I've seen kingdoms rise and fall,
But without you, they mean nothing at all.
This emptiness, a heavy weight,
A lingering shadow of a cruel fate.

The stars may shine, the moon may glow,
But they can't mend what I long to know.
A heart unclaimed, a love unspoken,
Leaves behind a soul that's broken.

For all I've gained, for all I've won
The truest loss is what's never begun.
A conqueror in the eyes of men,
But in love, a wanderer lost again.

This throne, this crown, they weigh me down,
For I've won the world but lost my ground.
And in the quiet of each night's regret,
Your absence writes the pain I'll never forget.

34. The Tale of Time

The story I lived, today it slips away,
Like whispers lost, in the cold light of day.
Every moment I chased, now starts to fade,
Like broken dreams, once bright, now decayed.

I held on tight, to what I knew,
But even the truest hearts must undo.
The warmth I sought, the love I craved,
Now leaves me cold, with my heart enslaved.

Tomorrow's promises seem so far,
As yesterday's memories leave a scar.
The battles fought, the tears I shed,
All fade into silence, words left unsaid.

I search, I beg, I fall, I scream,
But time keeps robbing, shattering dreams.
The love I gave, the hope I held,
All swept away, in a storm unpeeled.

So much I have lost, so much I gave,
Now lies in pieces, deep in the grave.
For every goodbye, a piece of me dies,
And I am left to wonder, how I survived the lies.

But still, I stand, though torn and bruised,
With a heart that is battered, and a soul that is used.
And in the pain, I somehow find,
A strength to leave what once was kind.

35. The Weight of Your Absence

You stand afar, I linger here,
A void too vast, a truth too clear.
Your memories strike like thunder's roar,
Each wave of thought breaks me more.

I've borne the pain, I've walked alone,
But how much longer can this heart atone?
You left me shattered, without a sign,
Tell me, will time ever make this fine?

The scars you gave, still carve my soul,
Perhaps your prayers could make me whole.
If heaven hears the cries of two,
Let its mercy flow from me to you.

I was not this man, broken and worn,
Life reshaped me, left me torn.
What was my sin, what was my crime,
To lose my way, to lose my time?

The smiles I wear are a clever disguise,
But you've seen the truth in my eyes.
The world sees joy; they never see pain,
Only you can feel my tears in the rain.

Say something, break this endless pause,
Your silence, to me, feels like a loss.
I see ruins where a home once stood,
I crave the warmth, the love, the good.

If nothing remains, no dreams, no part,
Let me rest where you buried my heart.
Beneath the soil, where silence sleeps,
Let me lie where my soul still weeps.

36. Twinkle - Twinkle Little Star

Twinkle - Twinkle little star,
Why should I wonder what you are?

How much you suffer to bring this light,
Are you fighting with this darkness, or you choose this night?

Do you also have some secrets to hide,
Are you also alone, or there is someone to be on your side?

Do you carry scars hidden from view,
Is the pain that I feel, known to you?

Do you stare at us, at times when we cry,
Will you please be my witness, once I die?

37. The Last Day

Not enough were there, to lift me away,
Not enough shoulders on my last, lonely day.

My friends, my own, all lost in the race,
Each tied to life's fast and frantic pace.

I lay there waiting, a journey to start,
Alone and abandoned, breaking apart.

In that cold silence, I felt the sting—
Left on the edge, just a forgotten thing.

No farewell whispers, no hands held tight,
Just empty shadows in fading light.

38. What If

What if, pain is why we live,
The heavy load we all must give?
What if, joy comes with a cost,
And happiness fades, leaving us lost?

What if, we go when we find the light,
Slipping away into the night?
Or what if, in death, we finally see,
The joy we lost and want to be free?

Each moment of sorrow, a step we take,
A path we walk, a choice we make.
In life's dance, pain and joy are near,
In every heartbeat, both are here.

39. A Silent Sacrifice

There are times in life when a choice must be made,
Between saving someone else or watching your life fade.
You give them your all—your peace, your grace,
Sacrificing your life to save their place.

As the years go by, someone asks you why—
"You haven't done anything," they say with a sigh.
You respond with silence, a heart that's torn,
"I gave up my everything, but still I mourn."

Yet they press on, "Why not try harder still?
You could have made it work, if you had the will."
And to that question, you say no more,
Just a smile that speaks of the battles you bore.

That smile holds the pain you couldn't share,
The tears that fell in a world so unfair.
It carries the screams that no one heard,
A silent story, without a word.

In that smile lies all you've lost,
The sacrifices made, the ultimate cost.
A life given away, piece by piece,
Wrapped in a smile that never finds peace.

40. Cycles of Light and Shadow

People say,
"If there's day, night will soon follow,
And after the dark, dawn breaks to glow."

But sometimes,
The night brings no day in its wake,
Only a dim light, a hollow ache.

Sometimes,
The rhythm shifts, cycles twist,
Bright nights stay, dark nights persist.

Sometimes the clock pauses, yet time slips away,
The sun longs to rest, to bid farewell to its ray.

We are demons in tales others spin,
Yet look at the heavens, still hoping to win.

People wish for compassion, looking at the sky,
But hardly take the first step, most don't even try.

41. A Question Unspoken

"Have you ever been in love?" she asked,
I paused, hiding pain behind my mask.
"Yes," I murmured, a distant ache,
I've felt love's warmth, then watched it break.

Held close just long enough to bruise,
Left alone with dreams I'd lose.
They came and left, no reason why,
And none stayed near to catch my cry.

No one saw the scars that grew,
The weight of love that never knew,
How deep it cut, how much it cost—
The love I gave, the love I lost.

42. Stand Alone

I know,
It's not easy.
It never was.

So, get up!
Take back every dream you've ever lost,
Because no one will fight your wars,
No one will light your path.

If you're still hoping for someone to arrive,
To pull you from this ocean, help you survive—
My friend, please wake up from that dream,
Life isn't as simple as it may seem.

No saviour is coming, no hand to guide,
You are the force that must rise inside.
The world is cruel, but you're strong,
You've carried this weight for so long.

So stand on your own, break free from the night,
Only you can turn darkness into light.
In your hands is the power to break through,
And everything you need is already in you.

43. Cycles of the Past

The past repeats, like a haunting song,
Pulling me back where I don't belong.
But love's gentle hand pulls me aside,
Breaking the cycle, turning the tide.

In every shadow, love plants a spark,
To guide me through the endless dark.
The chains of the past lose their might,
In love's embrace, I find my light.

44. A Prayer for Peace

Dear God, I lack the mind to see,
The depths of all Your plans for me.
I trust in You, with heart and soul,
To guide me where I need to go.

But God, right now it's hard to bear,
The weight of all this pain and care.
Whatever's happening, day by day,
It's hurting more than words can say.

Please, I ask, just grant me peace,
A moment where the pain can cease.
I'll trust You still, and follow through,
But calm my heart, I beg of You.

45. Let Me Die

Let me die, I whispered in the night,
When shadows loomed, and love was out of sight.
But a gentle voice within me spoke,
A thread of love, unbroken, woke.

Though despair held me in its cruel clasp,
It was love's faint light that helped me grasp,
That even in darkness, love still survives,
And in its warmth, broken hearts revive.

Let me live, I whisper anew,
With love's soft glow guiding me through.

46. It's Okay to Not Be Okay

It's okay
to not feel okay at all times.
Sometimes the weight of the world
crushes our hopes and dreams,
leaving us tangled in chaos,
lost in a silent scream.

Yet in moments of pain,
when shadows swallow the light,
remember that it's a reminder
you're still alive to fight.
Through the storms that rage inside,
and the tears that carve your face,
there's beauty in the struggle,
a raw and sacred grace.

Every struggle has a story,
every mark shows how we've grown.
In the depths of our sorrow,
we discover we're not alone.

So, embrace the ups and downs,
and know it's part of the way—
it's perfectly okay
to not be okay.

47. The Unattainable Hero

You won't be the sun in every sky,
Nor the warmth every soul will seek.
Some will find fault where others find grace,
For every heart reads you unique.

In someone's tale, you're the villain,
In another, just a fleeting name.
For a few, you're a treasure of love,
But for others, you're a spark of blame.

Not all hearts will open to you,
Not all eyes will see your light.
And that's the truth of this journey,
You can't be perfect in every sight.

Embrace the love, endure the hate,
For balance is life's eternal trait.

48. The Balance of Life

Perfection is a distant star,
We chase it, yet it stays afar.
Each solution births a fresh demand,
Life's riddles shaped by fate's own hand.

The light shines bright against the night,
Joy is born from sorrow's fight.
Without the dark, what's left to see?
Even bliss would cease to be.

So learn to loosen, let things flow,
Accept the things you can't control.
For grasping tight, you'll only find,
Life slips like sand, no peace of mind.

49. A Gentle Call

The sun has risen, warm and bright,
Casting hope, a tender light,
A gentle call to end the night.

Why linger still, while morning's here?
Wake up now, your path is clear.

The day awaits—just give it a try,
It's time to spread your wings and fly.

50. The Cost of Every Choice

Doesn't matter if you rise or fall,
Life demands a price from all.
Every step, each path we take,
Carries a cost, a toll to stake.

Victory's joy or defeat's sting,
Both come tied with their own string.
A silent fee, we can't evade,
For every move, the dues are laid.

So walk your journey, come what may,
The cost is life's inevitable way.

51. Fireflies and the Sun

The fireflies dance, their glow so small,
A light that flickers, soft for all.
It shines at night without a strain,
No loss, no hurt, no lasting pain.

But the sun must blaze with all its might,
To keep the world bathed in its light.
It fades, it burns, day after day,
Giving itself to light our way.

For every glow that changes sight,
There's always one who pays the price.

52. Broken Yet Strong

You may be broken, shattered as hell,
Yet in each crack lies a story to tell.
Strength in silence, resilience unseen,
the quiet warrior you have always been.

For in the fragments, there's something new,
A version of you that only you knew.
A difference so deep, yet hard to see,
A quiet resilience, a silent plea.

People may overlook what you've become,
But in your brokenness, you've quietly won.
What they can't grasp, you'll always know—
It's in the cracks where the strongest things grow.

53. Resilience in Darkness

At certain moments in life,
when it feels like all hope has fled,
and shadows wrap around your head,

Remember,
even in the depths of despair,
there's always a spark that lingers,
a whisper urging you to care.

Look closely;
something precious remains,
a memory, a hidden dream,
a chance to break the chains.

So dare to try,
to rise from the dark,
before nature brings its tears,
and dims your inner spark.

For within you lie the strength
to face the coming dawn,
to embrace each new beginning
and let your spirit carry on.

54. Choosing Hope

In quiet corners of our minds,
Where shadows often roam,
There lies a light we sometimes miss,
A place we can call home.

Hope isn't always handed down;
It's found where paths divide—
A whisper when all falls apart,
A choice we make inside.

When skies grow dark and doubts creep in,
And dreams seem far away,
Hope is the fire we choose to feed,
To guide us through each day.

So hold it close, this steady spark,
And let it guard your soul—
For hope, once chosen, stands unshaken,
The strength that keeps us whole.

55. The Power Within

The wounds we carry, the scars we hide,
Can heal if we let hope reside.
Forgive the pain, release the weight,
Choose to grow, it's never too late.

The mind can mend, the heart can too,
With every step, we're born anew.
Trust your strength, let healing start,
The power lies within your heart.

56. Light in the Darkness

If life feels empty and you find it is of no worth,
Then live for those who need your warmth on this earth.
If love and kindness never came your way,
Be the one who gives it, day by day.

For meaning grows, where hearts are healed,
In every act of love revealed.
What you don't receive, you can always share,
In giving, you'll find yourself somewhere

So when you feel empty, lost in the night,
Be the one who shares the light.
In giving love, you'll find your part—
A life of meaning, a generous heart.

57. Keep Smiling

Keep smiling.
Not everyone deserves to see your tears.

Those who truly care
will never make you cry.
They'll stand by your side,
until your eyes run dry.

In their embrace, find comfort,
in their love, find your way.
Hold on to those who care,
and let them brighten your day.

58. The Light in the Shadows

Sometimes, it's darkness
that keeps us alive,
A shelter from storms,
where hope can survive.

Unknowingly, we crave
for the light to appear,
Praying for betterment,
to conquer our fear.

We seek out perfection,
a life that feels right,
Yet in the deep shadows,
we discover our light.

So embrace the darkness,
let it teach you to fight,
Sometimes, it's in shadows
we find what feels bright.

59. A Happy Sunset

The sky ignites with crimson and gold,
A story of love, timeless and bold.

In every glow, a hope reborn,
In the shadows of night, dreams are born.

Through gentle winds, our hearts are set,
On paths that lead to a happy sunset.

60. The Mountain of Life

Life is a mountain, towering and steep,
A climb so many are eager to keep.
To reach its top, we're told to give,
To sacrifice much, for the life we live.

We trade away sleep, peace, and rest,
Our happiness, time, and all we invest.
Even health and dreams, we leave behind,
Chasing the goals that fill our mind.

But one thing, should never be used as a step,
Please don't sacrifice people to get ahead.
For relationships to breathe, they feel and grow,
With souls as deep as rivers flow.

Hold close those bonds, through every climb,
For they're the treasures we leave behind.

61. Trust the Flow

Not every fish that drifts along
Is lifeless, weak, or simply wrong.
Sometimes, life demands we move,
Through intense currents, we must approve.

There are moments we can't resist,
The flow is too strong, the force persists.
Not from defeat, nor lack of will,
But trusting fate to guide us still.

When paths diverge, and storms are near,
When choices blur and hearts feel fear,
It's then we lean on plans unseen,
For what will be, must intervene.

The easy road may seem so bright,
Yet hides its trials beyond the light.
While rocky trails, though rough and steep,
May lead to joy, profoundly deep.

For what we lose, or yearn to gain,
May shield us from an unseen pain.

And gifts we cherish, born from strife,
Might someday become the heart of life.

So trust the flow when doubts arise,
Let go of tears, release the whys.
In Krishna's hands, let burdens stay,
A sarthi guiding night and day.

For in this trust, we find our way,
Through waves that crash, and skies that grey.
We're not dead fish, but wise, alive,
With faith in God, we'll surely thrive.

62. The Flame's Secret

Not everyone can be a flame,
Burning bright, yet hiding pain.
Giving light to those in need,
While their own heart continues to bleed.

Imagine the shadows they must hide,
The silent tears, the storm inside.
To shine for others, they fade away,
Turning their nights into someone's day.

But who will light their darkened soul?
Who'll mend the parts no longer whole?
For even the brightest need some care,
A gentle hand to be their flare.

63. A Love That Heals

In every wound, love plants a seed,
It gives us strength in times of need.
When hearts are bruised, and spirits low,
Love whispers softly, "Let me grow."

It's in the smiles we freely give,
The little acts that make us live.
Through love, we mend, we rise, we heal,
It helps us learn; it makes us feel.

No chain can bind, no storm can break,
The power of love for love's own sake.
It turns the pain into something new,
A guiding light that sees us through.

64. The Light Within

In a world that's often cold and grey,
You hold the power to brighten your way.
With every thought, a seed you sow,
The garden of your mind will grow.

Choose kindness, let it lead,
Nourish your soul with every deed.
What you give is what you gain,
Sunshine follows after rain.

Embrace your flaws, let them guide,
They're the beauty you don't need to hide.
Self-love is the strongest shield,
In its warmth, all wounds can heal.

The vibes you carry, the love you share,
Shape your life with tender care.
So rise each day, let your spirit thrive,
For joy is yours when good vibes drive.

65. Flickers of Light

In a world of shadows, we sometimes walk,
Where whispers of sorrow echo as we talk.
Yet, even in darkness, bright places rise,
A quiet glow beneath the skies.

We meet souls who shine, despite their fight,
Who carry storms, but still spread light.
They teach us that pain can also guide,
To brighter days where hope resides.

Though some may fade, their glow remains,
A lasting warmth through life's domains.
For every scar and tear we face,
There's still beauty in every place.

66. Learn to Forgive

Please,
Learn to forgive, let go of the pain,

For holding onto bitterness brings nothing but strain.

Believe me or not, life's far too brief,
To live in anger or carry disbelief.

Spend your days with those you adore,
Share your love, and cherish more.

Because at the end, when all fades away,
It's the love we shared that will forever stay.

67. Trust the Process

How relative our lives truly are,
Each wound we bear, each inner scar.
The weight of pain we hold inside,
Is scaled by traumas we've survived.

We chase the bubble of fragile cheer,
A fragile hope that soon disappears.
And sometimes, life feels far from peace,
A living hell masked by life's ease.

When you're empty yet carry it all,
Standing at the edge, ready to fall,
Remember, someone out there too,
Holds deeper wounds than those in you.

In those moments, trust your way,
Trust the path, come what may.
Say, "God, I trust in what you've planned,
Hold me steady, guide my hand."

68. When Sense Unfolds

Whatever unfolds in your life today,
Happens for reasons, though hidden, they say.
You may not see the cause or the why,
But trust in time as answers come by.

Each trial, each tear, has a role to play,
Guiding your steps in its quiet way.
And soon the chaos will all make sense,
A story of growth, not just suspense.

69. The Inner Strength

Try to find your inner light,
For in your darkest, loneliest night,
No one will stand beside your pain,
With you, for you, through the rain.

And even if someone is near,
You'll be too lost to see them clear.
The darkness blinds, the pain's too deep,
No comfort found, no peace to keep.

So work hard now, before that day,
When all will leave and walk away.
Hold yourself when you're alone,
When the world breaks you to the bone.

Close your eyes and make a vow,
"I will be strong, I will rise somehow.
No matter what, I will hold on—
I have to be, I will be strong."

70. Remembering the Past

Never forget what others have done,
The kindness shared; the battles won.
Hold close the memories, both good and bad,
Every moment shapes the path we've had.

But also remind them of what's been real,
The gifts they gave, the wounds that heal.
Some acts are deep, they leave a mark,
A light in the night, a spark in the dark.

So cherish the ties that bind us tight,
And share the truths that bring us light.
In every heart, let gratitude grow,
For the love we've known and the pain we show.

71. The Roads We Cannot See

At every turn, a choice unfolds,
A mystery the future holds.
What if I'd stayed, what if I'd gone?
Would I still find where I belong?

In one life, joy, in another, pain,
Each decision, sunshine or rain.
Paths diverge, yet hearts remain,
Seeking love through loss and gain.

We dream of lives we didn't choose,
Of battles won and those we lose.
But even in the darkest night,
Each path we walk still holds its light.

For every ending, there's a start,
A lesson learned, a growing heart.
So here I stand, with open eyes,
Embracing fate, no need for whys.

72. The Cycle We Break

I stood in the storm, a heart torn apart,
Wrestling with love and the weight it imparts.
Dreams once painted in colours so bright,
Now faded to shadows, lost in the night.

They say love should heal, not leave scars,
But sometimes it wounds, and dims the stars.
The warmth that once felt like home's embrace,
Can turn into a battle, a silent chase.

Yet strength is born in the quietest pain,
In choosing to walk through the heaviest rain.
To break the chain, to stand and say,
"This hurt won't define me another day."

Love's not a wound, nor a fleeting game,
It's a chance to rise, to feel whole again.
And though the past may still haunt and ache,
The future is ours—new paths to take.

73. A Promise in the Dark

I am a lightless soul, roaming a darkened sky,
A wingless bird, who is daring to try—to fly.

Though storms may come, and shadows cry,
I will not break; I will not die.

I carry promises, close to my heart,
Dreams to fulfil before I depart.

So here I'll stand, through shadows and flame,
Until my journey justifies my name.

74. The Cost of Love

I loved, I lost,
My heartbeats bore the cost.
Each rhythm speaks, each echo cries,
Of tender truths and bitter ties.

I gave my all, no second thought,
Yet in the end, it came to nought.
The love I held, so deep, so true,
Now fades softly, like morning dew.

But though it aches, this fragile chest,
I know my heart has done its best.
For love, though passing, leaves its mark,
A gentle glow in shadows dark.

I loved, I lost,
But I won't count it as a cost.
For every beat, though torn apart,
Still proves the strength of a loving heart.

75. Love in the Stars

In the vastness of the night sky, we met,
Two souls adrift, lost in a world of regret.
But in your eyes, I found the truth untold,
A love like fire, against the chill, so bold.

We spoke of dreams, and whispered fears,
Of fleeting time, and uncried tears.
In the face of sorrow, we learned to fight,
Finding beauty even in the darkest night.

We held each other, in moments so brief,
A lifetime carved in a single shared belief.
That love, though fragile, burns ever bright,
A flicker in the dark, defying the night.

No promises made, no future guaranteed,
Just the bond we had, and the love we need.
For in this world of questions and unknowns,
It's the love we give that turns us to stone.

So let the stars burn, let the sky fall apart,
In the end, it's your memory I'll keep in my heart.
For love, like the universe, forever expands—
A truth that time cannot erase from our hands.

76. The Choice of Emotion

In pain, I sometimes choose to stay,
A heavy weight that won't fade away.
Happiness slips like morning light,
It fades too fast, out of my sight.

Both joy and pain depend on the day,
Laughter comes and goes, in its own way.
But I'll try to find a spark inside,
Even in darkness, I will not hide.

Though the winds may twist and bend,
I know that peace is not pretend.
In every heartbeat, I'll find my way,
To keep my smile, come what may.

77. The Fight

I fought the battles within my soul,
The endless waves, the crushing toll.
But love stood firm, a guiding flame,
Through every struggle, it called my name.

Love whispered strength when I felt weak,
It held me up when words couldn't speak.
In love, I found the will to fight,
To stand my ground and seek the light.

78. Her Promise

I know the pain you've carried long,
I see the battles, what feels wrong.
I know the tears that fall each night,
I understand why you can't fight.

But trust yourself, you've come so far,
Have faith in us, no matter how hard.
One day, we'll build a world that's kind,
A place of peace for heart and mind.

We'll make it better, wait and see—
A world where hearts can just be free.
We will, I promise— have trust in me.

79. Love's Second Bloom

They say the heart can only break,
Yet here I stand, for love's own sake.
A wounded soul, once torn apart,
Now dares again to risk its heart.

The echoes of a love long gone,
Still, hum like a sad song.
But in the silence, soft and new,
A tender hope begins to brew.

Scars remind, but they don't bind,
A fragile heart, now redefined.
For even in the deepest pain,
The seeds of love can bloom again.

So here I am, no fear, no shame,
Ready to kindle that old flame.
To trust once more, to let love in,
And start anew, where dreams begin.

End Note

As this journey through love comes to a close, I hope these poems have resonated with your heart in some way. Love, as we've seen, is not always gentle. It often tests us, breaks us, and forces us to confront our deepest fears. But it also teaches us resilience, the power of hope, and the courage to heal.

Through the moments of detachment and heartbreak, we discover our own strength. And in the process of healing, we learn that love, though once lost, can find its way back—sometimes in unexpected forms, sometimes with a familiar face, but always with a lesson we carry forward.

This collection ends where new beginnings take root—in the second bloom of love, where fear gives way to trust, and past wounds become the foundation for a stronger, more resilient heart. Love remains the driving force of life, not because it is perfect, but because it reminds us to grow, to endure, and to believe in the possibility of joy once again.

Thank you for sharing this journey with me. May these words stay with you as a reminder that even after love fades, it can return, bringing with it the promise of a new beginning.

So, in tough times, just remember:*Hope is a ray of light that keeps the magic of love alive.*

If these poems touched your heart, I'd love to hear from you. Follow my journey and share your thoughts on Instagram: @vg347_writes

About The Author

Physics in mind,
Love is in my heart,
Music flows in my arteries,
Poetry is the building block of my soul;

It's my family who ties up everything,
Adding life to this celestial body,
Making it a human, by making it whole…
VIVEK GUPTA ♥

Note To Reader

Dear Reader,

I hope you're happy, that your heart is light,
That you're smiling softly in the quiet of night.
But this note is for times when storms may rise,
When you're hurting deep, but don't show it in your eyes.

In those moments, remember this:
There are souls who care,
who'd miss each smile that you share.

God loves you beyond all measure,
More than you love yourself, beyond earthly treasure.
Even if you're upset with Him—it's okay, we all have the right—
But He alone knows the reason for each long, painful night.

So don't lose hope; keep faith, my friend,
Believe in the process, on Him depend.

We're travellers, passing through these days,
And this journey is too short to waste in greys.
Live with love, for those you hold near,
For at the day's end, it's them who'll keep you here.

Remember always, you're stronger than they see,

Much more resilient than you feel you could ever be.
And never forget—you're never alone,
You carry the warmth of loved ones, even if unknown.

With Love

- A Friend from Cosmos -

www.ingramcontent.com/pod-product-compliance
Lightning Source LLC
Chambersburg PA
CBHW031445150726
47990CB00007B/2624